Mysterious Rainforests

LIBRARIES NI
WITHDRAWN FROM STOCK

KINGFISHER

KINGFISHER

First published 2016 by Kingfisher
an imprint of Macmillan Children's Books
20 New Wharf Road, London N1 9RR
Associated companies throughout the world
www.panmacmillan.com

Copyright © Macmillan Publishers International Ltd 2016

Interior design by Tall Tree Ltd
Cover design by Peter Clayman

Adapted from an original text by Andrew Langley
Literacy consultants: Kerenza Ghosh, Stephanie Laird

Illustrations by Barry Coucher and Gary Hanna/www.the-art-agency.co.uk, Peter Bull Art Studio

ISBN 978-0-7534-3964-7

All rights reserved. No part of this publication may be reproduced, stored in or introduced
into a retrieval system, or transmitted, in any form or by any means (electronic, mechanical,
photocopying, recording or otherwise), without the prior written permission of the publisher.
Any person who does any unauthorized act in relation to this publication may be liable to
criminal prosecution and civil claims for damages.

Printed in China

9 8 7 6 5 4
4TR/0917/WKT/UG/128MA

A CIP catalogue record for this book is available from the British Library.

This book is sold subject to the condition that it shall not, by way of trade or otherwise, be lent,
resold, hired out, or otherwise circulated without the publisher's prior consent in any
form of binding or cover other than that in which it is published and without a similar
condition including this condition being imposed on the subsequent purchaser.

Picture credits
The Publisher would like to thank the following for permission to reproduce their material.
Top = t; Bottom = b; Centre = c; Left = l; Right = r
Front Cover Shutterstock/Eduardo Rivero, Shutterstock/szefei; Back cover Shutterstock/Anan Kaewkhammul;
Pages 4tl FLPA/Kevin Schafer; 4cl Ardea/Thomas Marent; 4tr Shutterstock/Rob Jenner; 4bl FLPA/Michael &
Patricia Fogden/Minden; 4br Nature/Shatti & Rozinski; 5tl FLPA/David Hosking; 5tr FLPA/Cyril Russo/
Minden; 5cr FLPA/Cyril Russo/Minden; 6l Shutterstock/Denis W.Donohue; 7bl Nature/Eric Baccega;
7tc Alamy/Kim Walls; 7tr Shutterstock/Piotr Gatlik; 8 Superstock/Juniors; 9 Shutterstock/Dr Morley Read;
10 Getty/Nigel Pavitt; 10 Photoshot/NHPA; 10tr FLPA/Gerry Ellis/Minden; 10c Getty/OSF; 11 Photolibrary/Sgm
Sgm; 11tl Shutterstock/Glen Gaffney; 11tr Superstock/Animals; 11bl FLPA/Mark Moffat/Minden;
11c Shutterstock/Lexan; 11br Shutterstock/Det-anan; 12–13 FLPA/Frans Lanting; 12tl Shutterstock/
ecoventurestravel; 12l Naturepl/Luiz Claudio Marigo; 12tr FLPA/Minden; 12br Shutterstock/Dr Morley Read;
13 Naturepl/Staffan Widstrand; 13b Shutterstock/Nicola Gavin; 14tr FLPA/Thomas Marent/Minden; 15 Ardea/
Thomas Marent; 16l Nature/Nick Garbutt; 16tr Alamy/Photoshot; 16c Photoshot/NHPA/ANT; 17cl Alamy/
Photoshot; 17b Photoshot/NHPA/Stephen Dalton; 18l Getty/Lars Hallstrom; 18t FLPA/Michael & Patricia
Fogden/Minden; 21cr FLPA/Luciano Candisani/Minden; 22 Corbis/Reuters/James Akena; 23tl Getty/David
Kirkland; 23c Superstock/Stock Connection; 23br Getty/Grant Faint; 24tl FLPA/Mark Moffett/Minden;
24bl Corbis/Erik de Castro/Reuters; 24c Shutterstock/Howard Sandler; 25cl Shutterstock/Hvoya;
24b Shutterstock/Hywitt Dywadi; 25b FLPA/Frans Lanting; 26–27 PA/AP; 27cl Getty/NGS; 27br Reuters/
Parth Sanyal.

Contents

Forest layers

Inside a rainforest, huge trees tower up into a mass of leaves high above. The air is hot and very humid, because there is heavy rain every day. The conditions are perfect for plants to grow – and these plants are home to a huge variety of animals.

The quetzal was worshipped by the ancient Aztec people, who lived in Mexico.

Canopy

A rainforest has several layers. At the top is the **canopy** of leaves. There is more sunlight up here, and the trees grow fruits and seeds throughout the year. Most animals live in the canopy, because there is plenty of food.

The Queen Alexandra's birdwing is the largest butterfly in the world, with wings up to 28 centimetres across.

Understorey

Stretching between the canopy and the ground is the **understorey**. Plants grow larger leaves to catch whatever light they can reach. With fewer branches, there is space for insects and birds to fly. **Reptiles** such as snakes move along the tree trunks.

The jaguar hunts for prey in rivers as well as on the forest floor.

The giant leaf-tailed gecko has a flat tail shaped like a leaf. It stands up and hisses loudly when threatened.

Forest floor

There is very little light here, and few plants can grow. Leaves and other litter fall from the trees above and cover the ground, where they rot down quickly in the humid conditions. Huge numbers of insects live among the **leaf litter**, including ants and termites. A few large **mammals**, such as anteaters and jaguars, hunt for food on the forest floor.

The mandrill is one of the most colourful of all mammals, with bright blue and red swellings on the face and rump.

The rafflesia plant has the world's largest flowers, up to 90 centimetres across. The plant produces a smell of rotting meat in order to attract flies that will **pollinate** it.

TOP FIVE BITESIZE FACTS

- More **species** of wildlife live in rainforests than in any other place on Earth.

- This **habitat** is under threat as areas are cleared for farms, mines and roads.

- Many canopy animals never go down to the forest floor.

- Only about 5 per cent of sunlight reaches the understorey.

- Tall trees poking above the canopy are called **emergents**.

humid
Moist or damp (in the air).

The world's rainforests

Most rainforests lie between the **tropics** of Capricorn and Cancer. Here the sun is hottest and the rainfall is highest. These are known as the tropical rainforests, but there are also temperate rainforests in cooler parts of the world.

NORTH AMERICA

The American black bear is one of the largest mammals living in the temperate rainforests of Canada and Alaska, USA.

KEY

temperate rainforest

tropical rainforest

AFRICA

Atlantic Ocean

Pacific Ocean

Amazon rainforest

Tropic of Capricorn

SOUTH AMERICA

Rainforest belts

There are three major belts of tropical rainforests across the world. The largest covers the basins of the Amazon and Orinoco rivers in South America. The others are along the Congo River in Africa, and from Myanmar to New Guinea in Southeast Asia.

temperate
Parts of the world that lie between the tropics and the polar regions.

6

The estuarine crocodile lives in saltwater areas on the coasts of Southeast Asia and Australia. It is the world's largest crocodile.

ASIA

The Iban people of Sarawak, Malaysia, build wooden longhouses on stilts that keep them high above river floods.

EUROPE

Southeast Asia

Tropic of Cancer

Pacific Ocean

AUSTRALIA

Indian Ocean

Equator

The massive Eastern lowland gorilla can be found only in the tropical forests of the Congo in Central Africa.

TOP FIVE BITESIZE FACTS

🌿 Temperate forests are kept damp not just by rain, but also by ocean or mountain fogs.

🌿 The biggest temperate rainforest is on the Pacific coast of North America.

🌿 Rainforests cover only 2 per cent of the Earth's total surface area, but are home to half of the planet's plants and animals.

🌿 The UK and Ireland would fit into the Amazon rainforest 17 times.

🌿 Plants in the Amazon rainforest produce more than 20 per cent of the world's **oxygen**.

On the floor

Barely any light reaches the rainforest floor where the canopy is thickest. Few plants grow here, and in some places the ground is bare except for a thin layer of dead leaves and twigs that have dropped from above.

Jungle giant

The African okapi is one of the tallest rainforest animals and it is related to the giraffe. It is nearly 2 metres tall, and can reach up to feed on the leaves of understorey trees.

invertebrate

An animal that does not have a backbone, such as an insect.

This trapjaw ant has the fastest-shutting jaws of all animals.

Plenty of food

The forest floor provides food and shelter for a huge number of insects. Ants and other invertebrates live in the leaf litter or in the soil. These in turn are eaten by spiders, centipedes and scorpions. Pigs and rats root among the litter. In turn, they are hunted by other animals higher up the **food chain**, such as snakes and big cats.

pupa of a trapjaw ant

TOP FIVE BITESIZE FACTS

- Less than 2 per cent of the Sun's light reaches the forest floor.

- The okapi has a tongue that is so long it can lick its own eyelids.

- Leafcutter ants chew up leaves into a mush. The **fungus** that grows on the mush is the ants' food.

- The Goliath bird-eating tarantula can grow to 30 centimetres across — as big as a dinner plate.

- The maiden's veil fungus gives off a foul smell to attract flies, which spread the fungus's **spores**.

Fantastic fungus

Fungi play an important part in the forest. They feed on plant tissue, and help break down the leaf litter. Mostly they are invisible, sending out tiny threads under the leaves, but occasionally they send threads up a stem or form structures that come in many shapes and colours.

maiden's veil fungus

leafcutter ant

The Goliath bird-eating tarantula is the largest spider in the world.

The understorey

The rainforest understorey is a mainly open space stretching from the floor up to about 20 metres – that's three times the height of a street lamppost. A few shrubs and small trees manage to grow here.

The tree kangaroo climbs by holding a branch with its front legs, then hops with powerful back legs.

The Burmese python has backward-sloping teeth that grip on to prey while the python's body crushes the prey to death.

On the up

The understorey is home to animals that can fly in the open spaces, or climb a short way into the trees. This includes a vast variety of birds, frogs, butterflies and other insects. The largest **predators**, such as leopards and snakes, blend in with the dappled shade of the plants as they hunt birds and small mammals.

TOP FIVE BITESIZE FACTS

- The Burmese python's strongest sense is smell. It uses its tongue to 'sniff' the air for prey.

- The Burmese python is one of the world's biggest snakes and grows to more than 5 metres long – about two and a half times the length of a bed.

- Inside its hairy skin, the rambutan fruit is soft, juicy and tasty.

- Flying foxes are the largest kind of bat and the biggest can weigh more than a kilogram – about the weight of a one-litre bottle of fizzy drink.

- There can be 500,000 weaver ants in a colony.

The clouded leopard is so called because its markings look like clouds.

Weaving leaves

In Southeast Asia, colonies of weaver ants make their nests with leaves. Starting at the tip, they fold over a leaf edge, clasp it with their jaws and 'sew' it to the other side. Their thread is a silky substance produced by the ant larvae (young that have just hatched). The ants squeeze the larvae gently so that they produce the silk that attaches one side of a leaf to another.

The flying fox is not a fox at all, but a fruit-eating bat.

Heliconia is a plant related to the banana.

The rambutan fruit is covered with fleshy spines.

colony
A number of creatures of the same species that live and work together.

The canary-winged parakeet has four toes on each foot (two facing forwards and two facing backwards), which help the bird cling to trees.

Crowded canopy

As well as the trees and their fruits, there are plants such as orchids, ferns and **bromeliads**, which grow in cracks in the trunks and branches. Many animals like to live in the safety of the canopy, where they find plenty of food.

Bromeliad leaves form a 'tank' that collects rain water.

The red howler monkey defends its territory by shouting and roaring.

A world in the air

The canopy is the roof of the rainforest. It can be 45 metres above the floor and forms an almost unbroken mass of leaves. The top part receives the full strength of the sunlight, but shades the areas below. Inside the canopy is a dense network of branches, vines and hanging plants.

The Amazon leaf frog keeps its eggs safe by wrapping them in leaves hanging over a river.

plumage
The feathers that cover a bird's entire body.

The three-toed sloth has fur that grows towards its spine, which allows rain to run off when the sloth hangs upside down.

The potoo has blotchy plumage and an unmoving stance that make it look like a tree branch.

TOP FIVE BITESIZE FACTS

- Many plant leaves are pointed so that rain water can run off easily and **algae** do not grow.

- Scientists estimate that 60 to 90 per cent of rainforest plants and animals are found in the trees.

- Animals living in the canopy have to fly, jump or glide across the gaps between trees to move around the treetops.

- Scientists studying the canopy build walkways from tree to tree to move around.

- **Lianas** are plants that climb up other plants and trees, using them for support.

The spider monkey hooks its tail over a branch.

When threatened, large mouth opens wide and head points towards the threat.

Tail grips branch while snake grabs prey.

Slim climber

The green vine snake comes down from the canopy to hunt mice or small birds, before climbing back up to rest.

Treetop travel

The rainforest canopy is not just a home, but also a highway for many animals. Monkeys, snakes, anteaters and even porcupines climb the trunks and travel along the branches. They have adapted so they can grab and cling to the trees and vines.

The fifth limb

Most climbing animals in the canopy have four limbs – two arms and two legs. But some, such as the South American spider monkey, have five. The fifth 'limb' is their long tail, which has a movable tip. The spider monkey can bend the tip over and use it as a hook for swinging on branches.

TOP FIVE **BITESIZE** FACTS

- The spider monkey's tail is so strong that it can hold the monkey's entire weight.

- Spider monkeys live in groups, called troops, with up to 40 members.

- Green vine snakes can be 2 metres long, but less than 1.5 centimetres thick.

- When attacking, the vine snake bites into the prey's head and lifts the victim off the ground so that it is helpless.

- The vine snake injects **venom** to paralyse its prey before swallowing it whole.

With its hands safe around the branch, the monkey then lets go with its tail and swings forwards.

Long arms reach out to grab another branch.

adapted
Changed over time to suit a new environment.

Feet that fly

All frogs have webs of skin between their toes, to help them swim. But some rainforest species, such as Wallace's flying frog, use these membranes to glide distances of longer than 10 metres. This flying frog lives high in the jungles of Borneo and Thailand in Southeast Asia.

Fliers and gliders

Many jungle animals appear only at night. Flying creatures, such as bats, look for food. Some animals have adapted to the dark. They cannot actually fly, but use flaps of skin to glide.

Tail steering

The female sugar glider of Australia glides through the air using membranes between her arms and legs, and steering with her tail. She has a pouch on her stomach in which her babies shelter.

Winged cradle

This colugo has a membrane that stretches from its shoulders to the tip of its tail. Spreading this out, the colugo can glide for over 100 metres. When she is not flying, the female colugo uses the membrane as a cradle for her young.

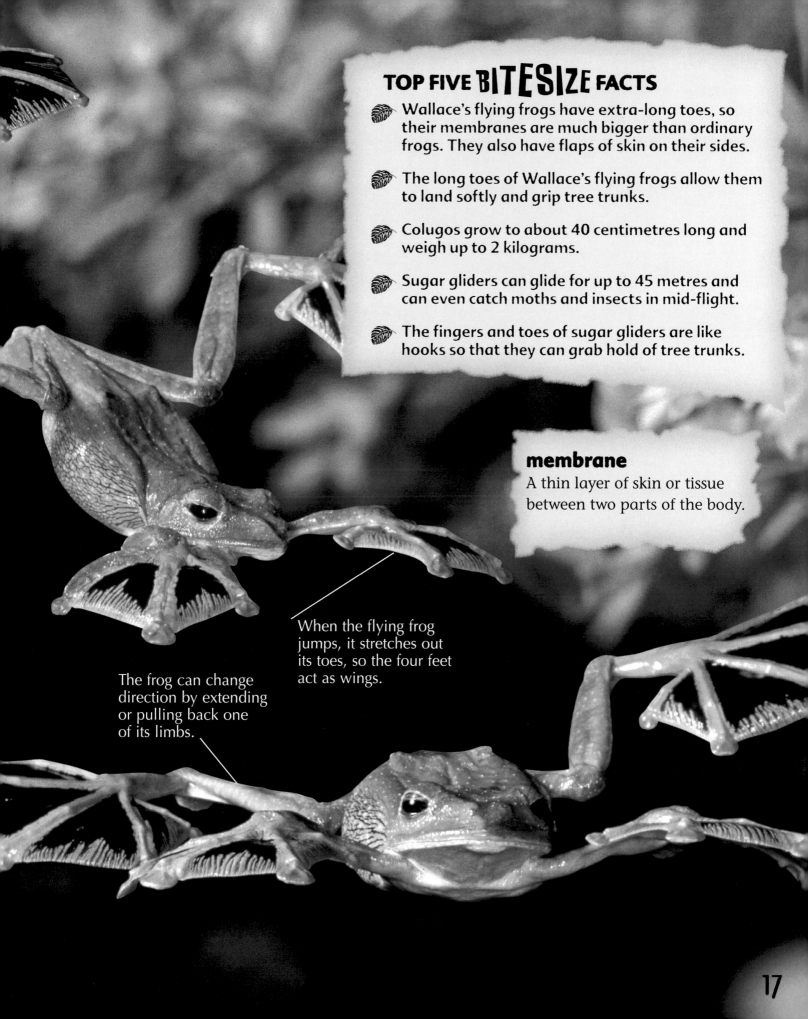

TOP FIVE BITESIZE FACTS

- Wallace's flying frogs have extra-long toes, so their membranes are much bigger than ordinary frogs. They also have flaps of skin on their sides.

- The long toes of Wallace's flying frogs allow them to land softly and grip tree trunks.

- Colugos grow to about 40 centimetres long and weigh up to 2 kilograms.

- Sugar gliders can glide for up to 45 metres and can even catch moths and insects in mid-flight.

- The fingers and toes of sugar gliders are like hooks so that they can grab hold of tree trunks.

membrane
A thin layer of skin or tissue between two parts of the body.

When the flying frog jumps, it stretches out its toes, so the four feet act as wings.

The frog can change direction by extending or pulling back one of its limbs.

Hunters and prey

There are few large hunters in the rainforest, and they are hard to spot. Hunters have to stay hidden, or their prey will see them. Leopards and other cats climb trees in search of food, or lie in the undergrowth. Other fearsome killers live on the forest floor.

Poison pump

The bushmaster snake of South America grows to more than three metres long. It has heat sensors on its head that detect warmth from other animals. Once it has caught the prey in its jaws, the snake injects deadly venom through its fangs.

Spotted coat mimics the dappled shade of the undergrowth.

Massive paws and sharp claws used to catch prey.

Death from above

The king vulture lives high in the canopy. It finds food by using its keen sense of smell, swooping on mammals or fish. Like other vultures, king vultures **scavenge** on dead creatures with their powerful beak.

prey
Animals that are killed and eaten by other animals.

Large ears pick up the slightest sound.

Four large canine teeth help to grip prey tightly.

Top cats

Cats live in the understorey of the rainforests. These are some of the biggest and strongest of all jungle animals. They are called 'top predators' because they have no natural enemies. The clouded leopard hunts monkeys and squirrels.

TOP FIVE BITESIZE FACTS

- The jaguar has the most powerful jaw muscles of all cats.

- A jaguar will ambush deer and other game animals by leaping from the ground onto their back.

- Once leopards have killed their prey, they will sometimes pull it up into a tree to keep it away from scavengers.

- Vultures have a bald head and neck. Any feathers here would get clogged with blood as the birds eat from the bodies of dead animals!

- King vultures build their nests on the ground.

Water life

Rainforest rivers provide a home for lots of living things. Plants such as giant water-lilies live here, as well as huge numbers of flies and other insects. There are also fearsome river hunters, including piranhas and caimans.

TOP FIVE BITESIZE FACTS

- Caimans have a see-through third eyelid which helps them to see while swimming underwater.

- Caimans can grow to 4 metres long — as long as a car.

- Piranhas have two rows of sharp teeth which they use to nip off chunks of flesh from their prey.

- The giant anaconda of the Amazon kills by wrapping its body around its prey and strangling it.

- Manatees can weigh as much as half a tonne — about the weight of an adult male polar bear.

piranha

A caiman lies half-hidden in the water, waiting to ambush its prey.

ambush
To attack something by surprise from a hiding place.

Capybaras are the largest rodents and have webbed feet. They live in groups of 20 or more.

River visitors

Many animals are attracted to rivers, because they are rich in food as well as water. Land animals come to drink, and swimmers visit to eat water plants or catch fish. Mammals such as capybaras or peccaries (a type of pig) make an easy meal for a caiman or snake.

River grazers

Manatees are large water mammals that eat mostly plants in shallow water. Manatees spend much of the day sleeping under water, coming up to the surface to breathe every 20 minutes.

Rows of special organs on each side of the eel's body release electric charges into the water.

Amazon electric eels can produce electric shocks to stun prey or use as a defence.

Rainforest people

Humans have lived in rainforests for thousands of years. They have learned to make the best of the rich resources that can be found there. Many of these people hunt and gather all they need from the forest around them. Some have never had contact with the outside world.

staple food
The major part of a person's diet – usually a starchy food, such as cassava or potatoes.

Hunting for food

The rainforests are difficult places to find food, but rainforest people have developed ways to survive. Some hunt animals for food. They use bows and arrows to shoot birds and monkeys, or nets and spears for larger animals such as deer.

A Ugandan pygmy hunts monkeys – a vital food source.

22

A village in one house

The Dayak people of Sarawak, Indonesia, have their homes in wooden longhouses. These are so big that a whole village of a dozen or more families can live together in one building.

Energy giving

Cassava (also called manioc) is a staple food of the rainforest people of South America and Africa. Its starchy roots grow well in poor soils and are a rich source of energy. Cassava is grated and crushed before cooking, to get rid of its poisonous juices.

TOP FIVE BITESIZE FACTS

- Hunters in the Amazon use **blowpipes** and coat the tips of the darts with poison from the arrow frog.

- It is estimated that 50 million people live in the world's rainforests.

- There are up to 500 different tribes living in the Amazon rainforest.

- About 50 of these tribes have never had contact with the outside world.

- Some tribes live as **nomads**, moving from one place to another to find food and shelter.

Ceremonial dress

Many people in the rainforest, such as this man from Papua New Guinea, decorate their body for special ceremonies. Decorations include body paint and large ornaments. These may indicate a person's importance, or act as charms to protect them from illness or bring good harvests.

Rainforest resources

Rainforests are full of many things that are vital to the planet. Some plants, such as rubber and cocoa, are now valuable crops. Many important medicines are produced from jungle plants. Spices, resins and dyes also come from the rainforest.

Climate change

A quarter of the world's carbon is 'locked' in rainforest plants. Humans burn vast areas of rainforest each year releasing carbon into the air. This adds to climate change, increasing natural disasters such as landslides and floods.

Flooding and landslides in the Philippines.

cocoa seeds

Researching the trees

Despite the hard work of scientists, there is still a lot we don't know about rainforests. For instance, how long is the full life cycle of a tree? There are no seasons in the tropics so trees do not show annual **growth rings**.

carbon
A substance that forms the gas carbon dioxide when trees rot down or are burned.

The biggest sugar cane-producing countries are Brazil and India.

Food crops

Many foods that you see or eat each day come from rainforests. Sugar cane originally came from the forests of New Guinea. Today, it is one of the world's most important crops. Other rainforest foods include coffee, cocoa, bananas, ginger and peanuts.

Coffee beans come from a tropical plant, and are now a major crop in South America and Southeast Asia.

Many plant species in tropical Kauai drifted to the island by sea and wind, or were carried by animals, including people.

TOP FIVE BITESIZE FACTS

- More than 170,000 square kilometres of rainforest are destroyed each year — that's the same size as the US state of Florida.

- Scientists have found more than 2000 tropical forest plants that have anti-cancer properties.

- In the past 50 years, almost one-half of the world's rainforests have been cut down.

- Chocolate really does grow on trees! Inside cocoa tree pods are the seeds from which cocoa powder and chocolate are made.

- 10 square kilometres of rainforest may contain 1500 species of flowering plant and 750 tree species.

The unknown

Every year, several completely new species of plants and animals are discovered, but many are still unknown to us. As the rainforests are gradually destroyed, these creatures may be lost for ever. Scientists examine and record the species they find. However, the area covered by the world's rainforests is so huge that much of it is unexplored.

Disappearing wilderness

Tropical rainforests began to disappear many thousands of years ago. Early humans learned to clear land with fire and tools. Over the centuries, the rate of the destruction has grown faster. Today, people use machinery to flatten the trees.

deforestation
The cutting down and destroying of trees and other plants in a forest.

Setting fire to the trees is a quick way of clearing a rainforest.

Map of destruction

As this world map shows, some regions of rainforest (marked with flame symbols) have been more badly hit by deforestation than others. Among the worst affected are Brazil and parts of Indonesia, where vast areas are still being destroyed today.

Smoking ruins

There are many reasons why forests are cut down. Farmers want more land to raise cattle or grow crops. Loggers want the timber from the trees to make paper and other goods. As populations grow, towns expand into areas that were once wild. But once the cover of the trees has gone, the soil quickly loses its **nutrients**. Heavy rains wash out all the goodness and cause erosion.

Super highway

Work on the Trans-Amazonian Highway in South America began in the 1970s. This giant road cuts straight through the rainforest. The Highway has opened up the area to even more logging and mining.

Cattle ranchers 'slash and burn' large areas of forest, and grow grass for herds of cattle to feed on.

TOP FIVE BITESIZE FACTS

- Cattle farming accounts for about half of all rainforest clearance.

- Rainforests are being cleared at a rate of one football pitch every single second.

- The number of Bengal tigers has actually increased in the past five years due to better management and protection.

- The Trans-Amazonian Highway is more than 5000 kilometres long.

- More than 70 per cent of the rainforest in West Africa has been destroyed.

Tigers in danger

As rainforests shrink and human settlements expand, many animals are losing their homes and hunting grounds. There are probably fewer than 2500 Bengal tigers alive today. They are being killed by **poachers** or by frightened villagers. This tigress was attacked when it strayed near a village in northeast India. It was rescued by forest workers, taken back into the rainforest and then released.

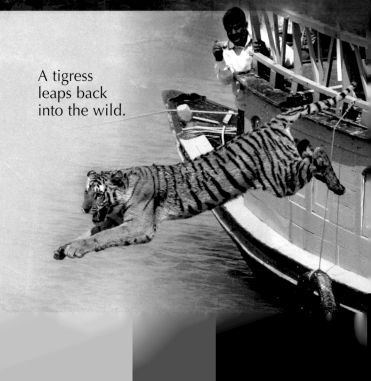

A tigress leaps back into the wild.

The last rainforests

Centuries ago, there were approximately 25 million square kilometres of rainforest across the globe. Today, almost half that vast area has gone – most of it in the past 50 years, due to human activity.

Hunting, war and habitat loss from farming, logging and charcoal production have reduced the number of red colobus monkeys.

Banana plantations, cattle ranching and logging have destroyed much of the great green macaw's habitat.

Populations of the golden lion tamarin, increased by conservation projects, live in small pockets of recovering forest.

Slow growth

In some countries, seedlings of rare rainforest trees are planted to reforest areas, but many trees grow very slowly. Mahogany trees can take several hundred years to mature.

TOP FIVE BITESIZE FACTS

- There are fewer than 2500 adult great green macaws left in Central America.

- The number of golden lion tamarins living in Brazil has increased from 272 in 1992 to more than 1000 today.

- There are only about 50 Javan rhinoceroses left in the wild.

- At the present rate of deforestation, the jungles of the world will have disappeared by 2060.

- There are fewer than 50,000 orangutans left in Southeast Asia,

extinct
No longer existing in a living form, having died out.

The Javan rhinoceros has lost habitat to farming and through poaching for its horn, which is valued in Asian medicine.

Chimpanzees suffer from poaching, disease and loss of habitat to farms, logging, oil and gas mining.

Loss of habitat to human interests (farms, roads, mines, settlements, logging, poaching) plus natural forest fires have had a bad impact on the numbers of orangutans.

Golden mantellas' habitat is threatened by logging, farming, settlements and fire.

Tourism has affected the habitat of this tree frog, and global warming makes its future uncertain.

Lost forever

The destruction of a rainforest harms far more than the trees. Mammals, birds, insects and reptiles lose their homes and food. These animals also disappear for good. Estimates show that 9000 species become extinct every year – most of them from rainforests. The destruction also threatens native peoples, who are driven out as the forests are cut down.

Glossary

algae
Single-celled plants that grow in water.

blowpipe
A long, narrow pipe through which a dart (small arrow) is blown.

bromeliad
A type of rainforest plant from the pineapple family that grows on trees.

canopy
The top layer of a rainforest.

emergent
A tree that sticks out above the canopy.

food chain
A series of living things that depend on each other for food. In the rainforest, a powerful predator such as a jaguar will be near the top of the food chain.

fungus
A type of living thing that does not have leaves, roots or stems and reproduces using spores.

growth ring
The layer of wood produced by a tree in a temperate region, showing one year's growth.

habitat
The surroundings that a plant or animal lives in.

leaf litter
Dead leaves that fall to the floor. Nutrients from the leaves pass back into the soil.

liana
A type of woody plant that climbs up other plants, using them for support.

mammal
An animal that gives birth to live young, which feed on their mother's milk.

nomad
A person with no fixed home, who wanders in search of food.

nutrients
Substances that living things need to absorb in order to live and grow.

oxygen
A colourless gas in the atmosphere that is necessary for plant and animal life.

poachers
People who hunt animals illegally, for their meat, skins, tusks or horns.

pollinate
To fertilize a plant by carrying a grain called pollen from a male plant to a

female plant. Pollen can be carried by wind, insects or other animals.

predator
An animal that hunts and kills other animals.

reptile
A cold-blooded animal with scaly skin, for example a lizard. Some reptiles lay eggs, but others give birth to live young.

scavenge
To feed on the bodies of dead animals.

species
A type of living thing.

spores
A cell, a bit like a plant's seeds, from which a new fungus grows.

tropics
Regions that lie on either side of the Earth's Equator.

understorey
The layer of a rainforest between the floor and the canopy.

venom
The poisonous fluid that some animals, such as snakes, inject into other creatures using fangs or stingers.

Index